RETHINKING RETIREMENT

T0375078

RETHINKING RETIREMENT

*Finishing Life for the
Glory of Christ*

John Piper

WHEATON, ILLINOIS

Rethinking Retirement

Copyright © 2009 by Desiring God Foundation

Published by Crossway
        1300 Crescent Street
        Wheaton, Illinois 60187

Originally published as "Getting Old for the Glory of God," in *Stand*, John Piper and Justin Taylor, general editors, copyright © 2008 by Desiring God.

Cover design: Chris Tobias

Cover illustration: iStock

First printing, 2009

Printed in the United States of America

Scripture quotations are taken from the ESV® Bible (The Holy Bible: English Standard Version®). Copyright © 2001 by Crossway, a publishing ministry of Good News Publishers. Used by permission. All rights reserved.

All emphases in Scripture quotations have been added by the author.

ISBN-13: 978-1-4335-0399-3
ISBN-10: 1-4335-0399-9
ePub ISBN: 978-1-4335-2305-2
PDF ISBN: 978-1-4335-0915-5
Mobipocket ISBN: 978-1-4335-0916-2

Library of Congress Cataloging-in-Publication Data

Piper, John, 1946–
    Rethinking retirement : finishing life for the glory of Christ
/ John Piper.
    Originally published as "Getting Old for the Glory of
God," in Stand, John Piper and Justin Taylor, general editors,
copyright 2008 by Desiring God Ministries—T.p. verso.
    Includes bibliographical references.
    ISBN 978-1-4335-0399-3 (tpb)
    1. Retirees—Religious life. 2. Retirement—Religious
aspects—Christianity. I. Taylor, Justin, 1976– . II. Stand.
III. Title.
BV4596.R47P57   2008
248.8'5—dc22   2009006440

Crossway is a publishing ministry of Good News Publishers.

VP		25	24	23				
15	14	13	12	11	10	9		

Finishing Life for the Glory of Christ

So even to old age and gray hairs,
O God, do not forsake me,
until I proclaim your might to
another generation,
your power to all those to come.

PSALM 71:18

Finishing life to the glory of Christ means finishing life in a way that makes Christ look glorious. It means living and dying in a way that shows Christ to be the all-satisfying Treasure that he is. So it would include, for example, not living in ways that make this world look like your treasure. Which means that most of the suggestions that this world offers us for our retirement years are bad ideas. They call us to live in a way that would make this world look like our treasure. And when that happens, Jesus is belittled.

Resolutely Resisting Retirement

Finishing life to the glory of Christ means resolutely resisting the typical American dream of retirement. It means being so satisfied with all that God promises to be for us in Christ that we are set free from the cravings that create so much emptiness and uselessness in retirement. Instead, knowing that we have an infinitely satisfying and everlasting inheritance in God just over the horizon of life makes us zealous in our few remaining years here to spend ourselves in the sacrifices of love, not the accumulation of comforts.

The Perseverance of Raymond Lull

Consider the way Raymond Lull finished his earthly course.

Raymond Lull was born into a wealthy family on the island of Majorca off the coast of Spain in 1235. His life as a youth was dissolute, but a series of visions compelled him to follow Christ. He first entered monastic life but later became a missionary to Muslim countries in northern Africa. He learned Arabic and after returning from Africa became a professor of Arabic until he was seventy-nine. Samuel Zwemer describes the end of his life like this, and, of course, it is the exact opposite of retirement:

> His pupils and friends naturally desired that he should end his days in the peaceful pursuit of learning and the comfort of companionship.
>
> Such however was not Lull's wish. . . . In Lull's contemplations we read . . . "Men are wont to die, O Lord, from old age, the failure of natural warmth and excess of cold; but thus, if it be Thy will, Thy servant would not wish to die; he would prefer to die in the glow of love, even as Thou wast willing to die for him."
>
> The dangers and difficulties that made Lull shrink back . . . in 1291 only urged him forward to North Africa once more in 1314. His love had not grown cold, but burned the brighter. . . . He longed not only for the martyr's crown, but also once more to see his little band of believers [in Africa]. Animated by these sentiments he

crossed over to Bugia [Algeria] on August 14, and for nearly a whole year labored secretly among a little circle of converts, whom on his previous visits he had won over to the Christian faith. . . .

At length, weary of seclusion, and longing for martyrdom, he came forth into the open market and presented himself to the people as the same man whom they had once expelled from their town. It was Elijah showing himself to a mob of Ahabs! Lull stood before them and threatened them with divine wrath if they still persisted in their errors. He pleaded with love, but spoke plainly the whole truth. The consequences can be easily anticipated. Filled with fanatic fury at his boldness, and unable to reply to his arguments, the populace seized him, and dragged him out of the town; there by the command, or at least the connivance, of the king, he was stoned on the 30th of June 1315.[1]

So Raymond Lull was eighty years old when he gave his life for the Muslims of North Africa. Nothing could be further from the American

---

[1]Samuel Zwemer, *Raymond Lull: First Missionary to the Moslems* (New York: Fleming H. Revell, 1902), 132–145.

dream of retirement than the way Lull lived out his last days.

Dying to Make Christ Look Great

In John 21:19, Jesus told Peter "by what kind of death he was to glorify God." There are different ways of dying. And there are different ways of living just before we die. But for the Christian, all of them—the final living and the dying—are supposed to make God look glorious. All of them are supposed to show that Christ—not this world—is our supreme Treasure.

So finishing life to the glory of Christ means using whatever strength and eyesight and hearing and mobility and resources we have left to treasure Christ and in that joy to serve people—that is, to seek to bring them with us into the everlasting enjoyment of Christ. Serving people, and not ourselves, as the overflow of treasuring Christ makes Christ look great.

The Fear of Not Persevering

One of the great obstacles to finishing life to the glory of Christ is the fear that we will not

John Piper

persevere in treasuring Christ and loving people—we just won't make it. We won't be able
to say with Paul in 2 Timothy 4:7–8, "I have
fought the good fight, I have finished the race,
I have kept the faith. Henceforth there is laid up
for me the crown of righteousness, which the Lord,
the righteous judge, will award to me on that Day,
and not only to me but also to all who have loved
his appearing." The reward of final righteousness
will come to those who have loved his appearing,
that is, who treasure him supremely and want him
to be here. So this treasuring of Christ must be
included in and part of the fought-fight and the
finished-race and the kept-faith. Faith includes
treasuring Christ and his appearing. You don't have
faith if you don't want Jesus.

So one great obstacle to finishing life to the
glory of Christ is the fear that we can't maintain
this treasuring of Christ. And so we fear that we
can't bear the fruit of love that flows from faith
(Gal. 5:6; 1 Tim. 1:5). We fear that we're not
going to make it. And the main reason that this
fear of not persevering in faith and love is an
obstacle to finishing life to the glory of Christ is

10

that the two most common ways of overcoming this fear are deadly.

Two Deadly Ways to Overcome This Fear

There are two opposite ways to ruin your life in trying to overcome this fear. One is to assume that perseverance in faith and love is not necessary for final salvation. And the other is to assume that perseverance is necessary and then depend on our efforts in some measure to fulfill that necessity and to secure God's favor. Let me show why both these are devastatingly misguided and deadly, and then what is the biblical way of finishing life to the glory of Christ.

Deadly: "Perseverance Is Unnecessary"

It's a mistake to think that perseverance in faith and love is not necessary for final salvation. A deadly mistake. Jesus said in Mark 13:13, "You will be hated by all for my name's sake. But *the one who endures to the end will be saved.*" Hebrews 12:14 says, "Strive for peace with everyone, and for *the holiness without which no one will see the Lord.*"

In Galatians 6:8–9, Paul says, "The one who sows to his own flesh will from the flesh reap corruption, but the one who sows to the Spirit will from the Spirit reap eternal life." So notice that the two reapings are of corruption on the one hand and eternal life on the other hand. Then he says in the next verse, "And let us not grow weary of doing good, for in due season we will reap [eternal life], if we do not give up."

So clearly persevering in the furrows of faith by sowing to the Spirit and bearing his fruit of love is necessary for final salvation. "God chose you," Paul says in 2 Thessalonians 2:13, ". . . to be saved, *through sanctification* by the Spirit and belief in the truth." "*Saved through sanctification*" means that sanctification—the path of love—is the path on which saved sinners go to heaven. And it's the only path that leads to heaven.

So it is a tragic and deadly mistake to try to overcome the fear of not persevering in old age by saying you don't have to persevere.

Deadly: "Perseverance Puts or Keeps God on Our Side"

But the other misguided way of overcoming the fear of not persevering is just as dangerous. It is the way that says: "Yes, perseverance in faith and love is necessary, and that means I must wait till the last day for God to be 100% for me, and I must depend on my efforts to secure God's full favor. God may get me started in the Christian life by faith in him alone, but perseverance happens another way. God makes his ongoing favor depend on my efforts." That, I say, is deadly and leads either to despair or pride. And certainly not to perseverance.

What's wrong with that? You can see what's wrong if you ask this question: When does God become totally and irrevocably for us—not 99%, but 100% for us? Is it at the end of the age, at the Last Day, when he has seen our whole life and measured it to see if it is worthy of his being for us? That is not what the Bible teaches.

What the Bible teaches is that God becomes 100% irrevocably for us at the moment of justification, that is, the moment when we see Christ as a beautiful Savior and receive him as our substitute punishment and our substitute perfection. All of God's wrath, all of the condemnation we deserve, was poured out on Jesus. All of God's demands for perfect righteousness were fulfilled by Christ. The moment we see (by grace!) this Treasure and receive him in this way, his death counts as our death and his condemnation as our condemnation and his righteousness as our righteousness, and God becomes 100% irrevocably for us forever in that instant.

"We hold that one is justified by faith apart from works of the law" (Rom. 3:28). "Therefore, since we have been justified by faith, we have peace with God through our Lord Jesus Christ" (Rom. 5:1). "There is therefore now no condemnation for those who are in Christ Jesus" (Rom. 8:1). So in Christ Jesus—in union with him by faith alone, by receiving all that he is for us—God is totally, 100% irrevocably for us. And the implications of that are spelled out in Romans 8:31–35:

> *If God is for us, who can be against us? He who did not spare his own Son but gave him up for us all, how will he not also with him graciously give us all things? Who shall bring any charge against God's elect? It is God who*

> *justifies. Who is to condemn? Christ Jesus is the one who died—more than that, who was raised—who is at the right hand of God, who indeed is interceding for us. Who shall separate us from the love of Christ?*

And the answer to that question is *Nothing!* Which means that all those who belong to Christ *will* persevere. They must, and they will. It is certain. Why? Because God is already now in Christ 100% for us. Perseverance is not the means by which we get God to be for us; it is the effect of the fact that God is already for us. You cannot ever make God be for you by your good works because true Christian good works are the fruit of God's already being for you.

"By the grace of God I am what I am, and his grace toward me was not in vain. On the contrary, I worked harder than any of them, though *it was not I, but the grace of God* that is with me" (1 Cor. 15:10). My hard work is not the cause but the result of blood-bought grace. "Work out your own salvation with fear and trembling, for it is God who works in you, both to will and to work for his good pleasure" (Phil. 2:12–13). Working out your salvation is not the cause but the result of God's working in us—God's being 100% for us. "I will not venture to speak of anything except what Christ has accomplished through me" (Rom. 15:18). If we are able to do anything by way of obedience, it is because Christ is already 100% for us.

If every exertion you make in the discipline of perseverance is a work of God, then these exertions do not make God become 100% for you. They are the result of his already being 100% for you. He is for you because you are in Christ. And you cannot improve on the perfection or the sacrifice of Christ. If by faith you are in Christ, God is as much for you in Christ as he will ever be or could ever be. You don't persevere to obtain this. Because of this, you *will* persevere.

So when the fear of not persevering raises its head, don't try to overcome it by saying, "Oh, there is no danger, we don't need to persevere." You do. There will be no salvation in the end for people who do not fight the good fight and finish the race and keep the faith and treasure Christ's appearing. And don't try to overcome the fear of not persevering by trying to win God's favor by your exertions in godliness. God's favor comes by grace alone, on the basis of Christ alone, in union with Christ alone, through faith alone, to the glory of God alone. He is totally, 100% irrevocably for us because of the work of Christ if we are in Christ. And we are in Christ not by exertions but by receiving him as our sacrifice and perfection and Treasure.

Overcoming the Fear of Not Persevering

So what is the right way to overcome the fear of not persevering in old age? The key is to keep finding in Christ our highest Treasure. This is not mainly the fight to *do* but the fight to *delight*. We keep on looking away from ourselves to Christ for his blood-bought fellowship and his help. Which means we keep on believing. We keep on fighting the fight of faith by looking at Christ and valuing Christ and receiving Christ every day.

Kissing Away the Fear

Charles Spurgeon said that God kisses away the fear of aging with his promises. Philippians 1:6: "I am sure of this, that he who began a good work in you will bring it to completion at the day of Jesus Christ." First Corinthians 1:8–9: "[He] will sustain you to the end, guiltless in the day of our Lord Jesus Christ. God is faithful, by whom you were called into the fellowship of his Son, Jesus Christ our Lord." Jude 24: "[He] is able to keep you from stumbling and to present you blameless before the presence of his glory with great joy." Romans 8:30: "Those whom he predestined he also called, and those whom he called he also justified, and those whom he justified he also glorified." No one is lost between justification and glorification. All who are justified are glorified. The point of telling us that is to kiss away all fear. If God is for us, no one can successfully be against us (Rom. 8:31).

The Key to Growing Old to God's Glory

Therefore, perseverance is necessary for final salvation, and perseverance is certain for all those who are in Christ. The works we do on the path of love do not win God's favor. They result from God's favor. Christ won God's favor. And we receive him by faith alone. And love is the overflow and demonstration of this faith.

This is the key to finishing life to the glory

of Christ. If we are going to make Christ look glorious in the last years of our lives, we must be satisfied in him. He must be our Treasure. And the life that we live must flow from this all-satisfying Christ. And the life that flows from the soul that lives on Jesus is a life of love and service. This is what will make Christ look great. When our hearts find their rest in Christ, we stop using other people to meet our needs, and instead we make ourselves servants to meet their needs. This is so contrary to the unregenerate human heart that it stands out as something beautiful to be followed or something convicting to be crucified.

It works both ways. Polycarp, the bishop of Smyrna, illustrates both and what it may mean for us to finish life to the glory of Christ.

The Perseverance of Polycarp

Polycarp was the Bishop of Smyrna in Asia Minor. He lived from about A.D. 70 to 155. He is famous for his martyrdom, which is recounted in *The Martyrdom of Polycarp*.[2] Tensions had risen

---

[2]The following quotes come from this account as translated and recorded in *Documents of the Christian Church*, ed. Henry Bettenson (Oxford University Press, 1967), 9–12.

between the Christians and those who venerated Caesar. The Christians were called atheists because they refused to worship any of the Roman gods and had no images or shrines of their own. At one point a mob cried out, "Away with the atheists; let search be made of Polycarp."

At a cottage outside the city, he remained in prayer and did not flee. He had a vision of a burning pillow and said to his companion, "I must needs be burned alive." The authorities sought him, and he was betrayed to them by one of his servants under torture. He came down from an upper room and talked with his accusers. "All that were present marveled at his age and constancy, and that there was so much ado about the arrest of such an old man." He asked for permission to pray before being taken away. They allowed it, and he was "so filled with the grace of God that for two hours he could not hold his peace."

In the town, the sheriff met him and took him into his carriage and tried to persuade him to deny Christ: "Now what harm is there in saying 'Lord Caesar,' and in offering incense . . . and thus saving thyself?" He answered, "I do not intend to do what you advise." Angered, they hastened him to the stadium where there was a great tumult.

The proconsul tried again to persuade him to save himself: "Have respect to thine age . . . ! Swear by the genius of Caesar . . . Repent . . . Say, 'Away with the atheists!' [that is, Christians]." Polycarp turned to the "mob of lawless heathen in the stadium, and he waved his hand at them, and looking up to heaven he groaned and said, 'Away with the atheists.'" Again the proconsul said, "Swear, and I will release thee; curse the Christ." To this Polycarp gave his most famous response: "Eighty and six years have I served him, and he hath done me no wrong; how then can I blaspheme my king who saved me?"

The proconsul said again, "Swear by the genius of Caesar." And Polycarp answered, "If thou dost vainly imagine that I would swear by the genius of Caesar, as thou sayest, pretending not to know what I am, hear plainly that I am a Christian." The proconsul replied, "I have wild beasts; if thou repent not, I will throw thee to them." To which Polycarp replied, "Send for them. For repentance from better to worse is not a change permitted to us; but to change from cruelty to righteousness is a noble thing."

The proconsul said, "If thou doest despise the wild beasts I will make thee to be consumed by fire, if thou repent not." Polycarp answered, "Thou threatenest the fire that burns for an hour and in a little while is quenched; for thou knowest not of the fire of the judgment to come, and the fire of the eternal punishment, reserved for the ungodly. But why delayest thou? Bring what thou wilt."

The proconsul sent word that it should be proclaimed aloud to the crowd three times, "Polycarp hath confessed himself to be a Christian." After the crowd found out that there were no beasts available for the task, they cried out for him to be burned alive. The wood was gathered, and as they were about to nail his hands to the timber he said, "Let me be as I am. He that granted me to endure the fire will grant me also to remain at the pyre unmoved, without being secured with nails." The fire did not consume him, but an executioner drove a dagger into his body. "And all the multitude marveled at the great difference between the unbelievers and the elect."

When we are so satisfied in Christ that we are

enabled to willingly die for him, we are freed to love the lost as never before, and Christ is shown to be a great Treasure.

A Charge to Baby Boomers

I am sixty-two years old—just about the oldest baby boomer (January 11, 1946). Behind me come seventy-eight million boomers, ages forty-three to sixty-one. Over ten thousand turn sixty every day. If you read the research, we are a self-centered generation.

> *Likes*: working from home, anti-aging supplements, climate control
> *Dislikes*: wrinkles, Millennial sleeping habits, Social Security, insecurity
> *Hobbies*: low-impact sports, uberparenting, wining and dining
> *Hangouts*: farmer's markets, tailgate parties, backyards
> *Resources*: $2.1 trillion[3]

What will it mean to finish life to the glory of Christ as a baby boomer in America? It will mean

---

[3] Accessed 9-27-07 at http://www.iconoculture.com/microsites/boomers/?gclid=COvX07OX5Y4CFSISQQod-x1QKQ.

a radical break with the mindset of our unbelieving peers. Especially a break with the typical dream of retirement. Ralph Winter is the founder of the U. S. Center for World Missions and, in his early eighties, is still traveling, speaking, and writing for the cause of Christ in world missions. He wrote an article titled "The Retirement Booby Trap" almost twenty-five years ago when he was about sixty. In it he said,

> Most men don't die of old age, they die of re-tirement. I read somewhere that half the men retiring in the state of New York die within two years. Save your life and you'll lose it. Just like other drugs, other psychological ad-dictions, retirement is a virulent disease, not a blessing. . . .
>
> Where in the Bible do they see [retire-ment]? Did Moses retire? Did Paul retire? Peter? John? Do military officers retire in the middle of a war?"[4]

Millions of Christian men and women are finish-ing their formal careers in their fifties and sixties,

---

[4]Ralph Winter, "The Retirement Booby Trap," *Mission Frontiers* 7 (July 1985): 25.

and for most of them there will be a good twenty years before their physical and mental powers fail. What will it mean to live those final years for the glory of Christ? How will we live them in such a way as to show that Christ is our highest Treasure?

The Perseverance of Charles Simeon

When I got prostate cancer and had surgery at age sixty, I recalled the experience of Charles Simeon and prayed that his outcome would be true for me.

Simeon was the pastor of Trinity Church, Cambridge, two hundred years ago. He learned a very painful lesson about God's attitude toward his "retirement." In 1807, after twenty-five years of ministry at Trinity Church, his health broke when he was forty-seven. He became very weak and had to take an extended leave from his labor. Handley Moule recounts the fascinating story of what God was doing in Simeon's life.

> The broken condition lasted with varia-
> tions for thirteen years, till he was just sixty,
> and then it passed away quite suddenly and

without any evident physical cause. He was on his last visit to Scotland . . . in 1819, and found himself, to his great surprise, just as he crossed the border, "almost as perceptibly renewed in strength as the woman was after she had touched the hem of our Lord's garment."

He says that he had been promising himself, before he began to break down, a very active life up to sixty, and then a Sabbath evening [retirement!]; and that now he seemed to hear his Master saying: "I laid you aside, because you entertained with satisfaction the thought of resting from your labour; but now you have arrived at the very period when you had promised yourself that satisfaction, and have determined instead to spend your strength for me to the latest hour of your life, I have doubled, trebled, quadrupled your strength, that you may execute your desire on a more extended plan."[5]

How many Christians set their sights on a "Sabbath evening" of life—resting, playing, traveling, etc.—the world's substitute for heaven since

---

[5]Handley C. G. Moule, *Charles Simeon* (London: The Inter-Varsity Fellowship, 1948, orig. 1892), 125.

the world does not believe that there will be a heaven beyond the grave. The mindset of our peers is that we must reward ourselves now in this life for the long years of our labor. Eternal rest and joy after death is an irrelevant consideration. When you don't believe in heaven to come and you are not content in the glory of Christ now, you will seek the kind of retirement that the world seeks. But what a strange reward for a Christian to set his sights on! Twenty years of leisure (!) while living in the midst of the Last Days of infinite consequence for millions of people who need Christ. What a tragic way to finish the last mile before entering the presence of the King who finished his last mile so differently!

The Perseverance of J. Oswald Sanders

When I heard J. Oswald Sanders at the Trinity Evangelical Divinity School chapel speaking at the age of eighty-nine say that he had written a book a year for Christ since he was seventy, everything in me said, "O God, don't let me waste my final years! Don't let me buy the American dream of retirement—month after month of leisure and play and hobbies and putzing around in the garage and rearranging the furniture and golfing and fishing and sitting and watching television. Lord, please have mercy on me. Spare me this curse."

Passion: Making God's Greatness Known to Future Generations

That is my prayer for you as well. I close with a passion and a promise. The passion is Psalm 71:18—a passion to make the greatness of God known to the generations we are leaving behind: "Even to old age and gray hairs, O God, do not forsake me, until I proclaim your might to another generation, your power to all those to come." O that God would give us a passion in our final years to spend ourselves to make him look as great as he really is—to finish life to the glory of Christ.

Promise: We Are As Secure As Christ Is Righteous and God Is Just

The promise: Isaiah 46:3–4, "[You] have been borne by me from before your birth, carried from the womb; even to your old age I am he, and to gray hairs I will carry you. I have made, and I will bear; I will carry and will save." Don't be afraid,

Christian. You will persevere. You will make it home. Sooner than you think. Live dangerously for the one who loved you and died for you in his thirties. Don't throw your life away on the American dream of retirement. You are as secure as Christ is righteous and God is just. Don't settle for anything less than the joyful sorrows of magnifying Christ in the sacrifices of love. And then in the Last Day, you will stand and hear, "Well done, good and faithful servant. . . . Enter into the joy of your master" (Matthew 25:21, 23).

desiringGod

Everyone wants to be happy. Our website was born and built for happiness. We want people everywhere to understand and embrace the truth that *God is most glorified in us when we are most satisfied in him.* We've collected more than thirty years of John Piper's speaking and writing, including translations into more than forty languages. We also provide a daily stream of new written, audio, and video resources to help you find truth, purpose, and satisfaction that never end. And it's all available free of charge, thanks to the generosity of people who've been blessed by the ministry.

If you want more resources for true happiness, or if you want to learn more about our work at Desiring God, we invite you to visit us at www.desiringGod.org.

www.desiringGod.org